6-31

Twist These On Your Tongue.

Twist These On Your Tongue

Joseph Rosenbloom

Illustrated by Joyce Behr

THOMAS NELSON INC., PUBLISHERS
Nashville • New York

First edition

Library of Congress Cataloging in Publication Data

Rosenbloom, Joseph.
  Twist these on your tongue.

  SUMMARY: A collection of tongue twisters arranged in alphabetical order.
  1. Tongue twisters. [1. Tongue twisters]
I. Behr, Joyce. II. Title.
PN6371.5.R614   818'.5'407   78-16776
ISBN 0-8407-6612-2

To Michael Halfon with love

Foreword

For a long time I was under the impression that tongue twisters were just for fun. I was wrong. Tongue twisters are part of our folklore heritage, and for this reason alone, they are worthy of being collected, edited, published, reviewed, and cherished.

While many of the items in the present collection are classic tongue twisters that have been passed down from generation to generation, and therefore may be considered as folklore, most are original creations of the author.

Imagine my pleasure, then, when I came across an alternative rationale for the tongue twister. One of the most authoritative encyclopedias in the English language recommends tongue twisters for use in:

(1) curing hiccups
(2) curing lisps and other speech defects
(3) testing the fit of dentures
(4) screening applicants for positions as broadcast announcers

Here were reasons weighty enough to justify tongue twisters to anyone. And yet, suppose the would-be tongue twister had no hiccups or special speech defects, wore no dentures, and was not especially interested in working as an announcer. What then?

After long and difficult research in the field—mind you, without so much as a single grant from the Ford or Rockefeller foundations—I hit on a startling sociological discovery: People who told each other tongue twisters had a tendency to resort to physical violence less frequently than those who did not. This could only mean one thing—namely that tongue twisters were important elements in the social bonding process!

I noted, moreover, that laughter frequently accompanied tongue twisters. And people in the grip of laughter are less inclined to punch, maul, or otherwise physically damage their fellow men than are the scowlers. Tongue twisters could obviously play a significant role in the reduction of social tensions and in enhancing feelings of group solidarity.

I am perfectly content with a view that empha-
sizes the profound sociological value of this form of
literature. If there are some who do not care for
such a notion, let them find their own excuses for
indulging in tongue twisters.

—J.R.

A

Ann Anteater ate Andy Alligator's apples,
and angry Andy Alligator ate Ann.

Assist a sister's sister assistant.

Had Tad the addled adder added ads?

"Is the axe's axis on the axle?" asks Axel.

"What ails Alex?" asks Alice.

B

Barbara burned the brown bread badly.

The barbarous Barbary barbarians bar Barbara with barbarity.

The barber barely barbers Bart at barbecues.

The barren baron borrows a bare blank black barrel.

Barry buys his blonde bride a bright-blue blowsy blouse.

A bawling batter blasts a baseball better.

Bea's yellow bumblebee bumps big blimps.

The beet that beat the beet that beat the other beet is now beaten by a beet that beats all the beets, whether the original beet that beat the beet or the beet that beat the beet that beat the other beet.

The best breath test tests breath better.

Betty Botter bought some butter.
"But," she said, "this butter's bitter.
If I put it in my batter,
It will make my batter bitter.
But a bit of better butter,
Will make my batter better."
So Betty bought a bit of butter,
Better than the bitter butter,
And made her batter better.

The big baker bakes black bread.

A big blocky blank block bank book.

A big blue bucket of blooming blueberries.

A big blue bug bit a big black bear,
Made a big black bear bleed blood,
As round the rough and rugged rock
The ragged rascal ran.

The bigwig's big wig bill is bigger.

Bill had a billboard.
Bill also had a board bill.
The board bill bored Bill,
So Bill sold his billboard
And paid his board bill.
Then the board bill
No longer bored Bill,
But though he had no board bill,
Neither did he have his billboard!

Bill is the best backward blowing bugler in the
Boston brass band.

A billion bulbous bulbs billow brilliantly.

Billy bought a better ball for baby.

Black Bart briefly bluffs.

Black bug's blood.

A blackened back box blocks Blanche.

Blabbing Bertha babbles barely boring baubles.

The bleak breeze blights the brightly blooming blossom.

The blind bugler blew a bigger bugle blast.

Blind Bea blinks back.

Blockheads blame big B-52 bombers.

A bloke's back brake block broke.

The bloke bled in the blue bed.

The blunted back blade is bad.

A blue-backed blackbird blew big bubbles.

The blunt beached bleached blonde bluffs.

Bobby Blue blinks at the back blank bank blackboard.

A bootblack blacks boots with a black blacking brush.

The bootblack brought the boot book back.

I bought a batch of baking powder and baked a batch of biscuits. I brought a big basket of biscuits back to the bakery and baked a basket of big biscuits. Then I took the big basket of biscuits and the basket of big biscuits and mixed the big biscuits with the basket of biscuits that was next to the big basket and put a bunch of biscuits from the basket into a box. Then I took the box of mixed biscuits and a biscuit mixer and brought the basket of biscuits and the box of mixed biscuits and the biscuit mixer to the bakery and opened a can of sardines.

Once upon a barren moor there dwelt a bear, also a boar. The bear could not bear the boar; the boar thought the bear a bore. At last the boar could bear no more the bear that bored him on the moor. And so one morn he bored the bear. The bear will bore the boar no more.

A box of biscuits, a box of mixed biscuits, and a biscuit mixer.

The brave brown bare bear barely bars brutally blunt bad bare bears.

A brown borrowed barrel bores brown borrowed burros.

Bruce brought baked black bread back.

The bug bag bugs buggy Bill Boggs.

A bunch of bad bloodthirsty bloodhounds block beached Bertha.

The bully billygoat bravely blasts the burly bull's bullish bliss.

Buy a bag of bright bleached blue-beaded blazers.

Does fussy Bea's fuzzy busy bee buzz busily?

Peggy Babcock blushes badly.

Red bug's blood and bed bug's blood.

Who bottled Blueblood's bad blood in two blue bottles?

Blueblood's blue bluebird.

Whose bored boar boards bores?

C

All I want is a proper cup of coffee,
Made in a proper copper coffeepot
You can believe it or not—
I want a cup of coffee
In a proper coffeepot.
Tin coffeepots or

Iron coffeepots,
They're no use to me.
If I can't have a
Proper cup of coffee
In a proper copper coffeepot,
I'll have a cup of tea.

As I was dashing down Cutting Hill,
A-cutting through the air
I saw Charlie Cutting sitting
In Oscar Cutting's chair,
And Oscar Cutting was cutting
Charlie Cutting's hair.

Can a clean clam cram clams in clean cream cans?

Can a counting count's accountant count count-less counters?

Can Cathleen cuddle Clara's cute colt closely?

Can Claire cue Carl's curtain call?

A canner exceedingly canny,
One morning remarked to his granny,
    "A canner can can
      Anything that he can,
But a canner can't can a can, can he?"

Can a clumsy clammy kid climb crags?

A chapped chap chops chipped chop tops.

Charlie Chip shops chop suey shops.

The cheeky chimp chooses cheese chip-dip
chunks.

Cheryl cheerfully chews choice chilled cherries.

A child's cheap chip shop sells cheap chips to
children.

Chief cheap sheep section.

Chop shops stock chops.

The chubby chess champ's chum cheats Charles.

Chuck chews and chews chicle chewing gum.

A chunk of choice cheap cherry-chip chocolate.

Cinnamon aluminum linoleum.

Claud's clunky clickety-clack, clippety-clop clogs clink.

Clear-cut clipped corners.

A clipper ship shipped several clipped sheep. Were these clipped sheep the clipper ship's sheep, or just clipped sheep shipped on a clipper ship?

A clump of Clem's clams clamped closed.

The cool, cruel schoolgirl's ghoul drools.

Coop up the cute cook!

The cranky crank cracks crackers crazily.

Crazy Craycroft caught a crate of
    crickled crabs.
Did Crazy Craycroft catch a crate of
    crickled crabs?
If crazy Craycroft caught a crate of
    crickled crabs,
Where's the crate of crickled crabs
    Crazy Craycroft caught?

The crocodile clears the close creek cleanly.

Cute crows clatter in cramped clothes closets.

Doctor Charles checks the cud-chewing cow's
chest chart carefully.

How many cookies could a good cook cook,
if a good cook could cook cookies?

I do like cheap sea trips,
Cheap sea trips on ships.
I like to be on the deep blue sea,
When the ship she rolls and dips.

I would if I could.
If I couldn't, how could I?
I couldn't if I couldn't, could I?
Could you if you couldn't, could you?

If you cross a cross across a cross,
Or cross a stick across a stick,
Or cross a stick across a cross,
Or cross a cross across a stick,
Or stick a stick across a stick,
Or stick a cross across a cross,
Or stick a cross across a stick,
Or stick a stick across a cross,
   Would that be acrostic?

The king closes a clutch of cruel
crew clubs.

D

A dear, daring, darling daredevil dared dive and dangle dangerously.

Do droves of drivers in drays dream of driving dried dead dreaded dragons?

Doubled bubble gum bubbles double.

A duke dragged a dizzy deacon down a deep,
damp, dark, dank den.

A dumb dumbwaiter dumps dumpy dumplings
on dumfounded dumbbells.

How much dew could a dewdrop drop if a dewdrop did drop dew?

A maid with a duster
   Made a furious bluster
Dusting a bust in the hall.
   When the bust it was dusted
The bust it was busted,
   The bust it was dust, that's all.

My dame had a lame, tame crane;
My dame had a lame, tame crane.
    Oh, pray, gentle Jane,
      Let my dame's lame crane
Pray drink and come home again.

When a doctor gets sick and another doctor doctors him, does the doctor doing the doctoring have to doctor the doctor the way the doctor being doctored wants to be doctored, or does the doctor doing the doctoring of the doctor doctor as he wants to doctor?

An expert ex–egg examiner exports experience.

Eight eager eagles ogle old Edgar.

Eighty-eight elder elegant elephants elope.

Ere her ear hears her err, her ears err here.

Esaw Wood sawed wood. Esaw Wood would saw wood. Oh, the wood that Wood would saw! One day Esaw Wood saw a saw saw wood as no other wood-saw Wood ever saw would saw wood. Of all the wood-saws Wood ever saw wood, Wood never saw a wood-saw that would saw like the wood-saw Wood saw would. Now Esaw saws with that saw he saw saw wood.

I saw Esau kissing Kate.
Fact is, we all three saw.
I saw Esau, he saw me,
And she saw I saw Esau.

F

False Frank fled Flo Friday.

Feed fresh fish food to frisky fish.

Few free fruit flies flock around flames.

The fickle finger of fate flips flat fat frogs.

A fine field of wheat,
A field of fine wheat.

The first fat fast master passed faster than the last
fat past pastor.

The fish-sauce shop's sure to sell fresh fish sauce.

Flighty fickle freckle-faced Freddie fidgets.

Flee from fog to fight flu fast.

The flesh of freshly fried fish.

A fly flew past Flo's flat,
And a fly flew past fat Flo.
Is the fly that flew past Flo,
The same fly that flew past fat Flo's flat?

For fresh shrimp, try a fresh shrimp shop.

The founding fathers fondle foundlings further.

Four famous fishermen found four flounders
faithfully following four floppy female flatfish.

Fresh Flora fixes front flats for friends.

Francis fries fish fillets for Frederick. Frederick
fillets fish for Francis' fried fritters.

Frank Fowler's friend flees from three free
fireflies.

French friars fanning five fainted fleas.

Friendly fliers flip-flop fairly freely.

Fruit float.

A furry frail fly flitted from friendly
flowing flower to friendly flowing flower.

A lively young fisher named Fischer
    Fished for fish from the edge
    of a fissure.
A fish with a grin
    Pulled the fisherman in.
Now they're fishing the fissure
    For Fischer.

Of all the felt I ever felt, I never felt a felt like
that felt felt.

Three fluffy feathers fell from feeble Phoebe's fan.

Three free-flow pipes.

You can have:
    Fried fresh fish,
    Fish fried fresh,
    Fresh fried fish,
    Fresh fish fried,
    Or fish fresh fried.

G

Cows graze in groves on grass which grows in
grooves in groves.

Gaze on the grim, grave brigade.

The geese group's great greased gander grows
grander in Greece.

George Gabs grabs crabs,
Crabs George Gabs grabs,
If George Gabs grabs crabs,
Where are the crabs George grabs?

Giddy girls giggle, gaggle, gargle, gurgle and
goggle.

Glen Green grows great gardens in glamorous
Glendale.

Good blood, bad blood.

The grape ape eats green grapes.

Great gray geese graze gaily daily.

Gwen glues glum Gwendolyn's glasses when glum
Gwendolyn glimpses Gwen.

H

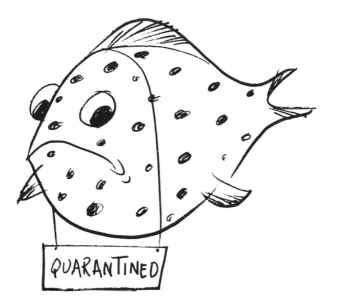

A haddock, a haddock, a black-spotted haddock,
A black spot on the black back of a black-spotted
haddock.

Hag Helga hales hag Hilga.

Harold hardly helps hard Hardy hurry Harry
home.

Hollow Helen Hill hobbles on hills.

Horrible Heidi hears hairy Horace holler.

If to hoot and to toot
　　A Hottentot tot
Was taught by a Hottentot tutor,
　　Should the tutor get hot
If the Hottentot tot
　　Hoots and toots
At the Hottentot tutor?

In Huron, a hewer, Hugh Hughes,
Hewed yews of unusual hues.
Hugh Hughes used blue yews
To build sheds for his ewes;
So his ewes a blue-hued ewed-shed use.

I

I see Isis' icy eyes.

The idle idol idolizes idleness.

Ike chips ice chips in ships.

Is it illegal to kill an ill eagle?

J

A gentle judge just judges justly.

Jail jaunty Jay gentle, Gene.

Jealous Jill's genuine jiggling jelly jells in a jumbo jigger jar or in a giant julep juice jug.

A jinxed jazzed-up cheap jeep jalopy generally jiggles, jumps, jars and jangles.

Junior's jolly June cheap sheep sleep soundly.

K

Clever Kate keenly cleans copper kettles.

Kay's key kindergarten class completes kid's kite kits.

Kick six sticks quick.

Kitty cuddles Clara's cute kitten carefully.

A knapsack strap.
A strap from a knapsack.

No known knight knits nine knots nightly not knowing knitting.

L

Lankey Lawrence lost his lass
    and lobster.
Did Lankey Lawrence lose his lass
    and lobster?
If Lankey Lawrence lost his lass
    and lobster,
Where's the lass and lobster Lankey
    Lawrence lost?

Lawless Lizzy laughs less listlessly.

Let level Lester list the last lesser lesson at least.

Lily lately ladled Lady Letty's lentil soup.

Loaded lowland llamas are ladylike.

The locale lacks a loco local locomotive.

Loony long-landlocked Lionel loves liver.

Lots of live lovelorn lonely lady librarians love loafing.

Lou licks eleven little licorice lollipops.

Louella is literally literary.

Lucid Lucy loves to lop lacy loose lace lumps.

M

A mad manager imagined he was managing a menagerie.

Marvin may muddle the marvelous middle melody.

Merry Mary marries Marty Monday.

I miss my Swiss Miss.
My Swiss Miss misses me.

Men munch much mush;
Women munch much mush;
Many men and women
Must munch much mush.

A missing mixture measure.

Marsha mostly ships cheap cherry marshmallows.

Miss Smith musses messy Mrs. Smith.

Mother's mellow miracle mustard makes most
moldy meat more munchable.

N

I need not your needles
   They're needless to me,
For the needing of needles
   Is needless, you see.
But did my neat trousers
   But need to be kneed,
I then should have need
   Of your needles indeed.

Nana's nimble needles knit nine narrow napkins.

Naughty Nelly nearly nudges noble Noel's nice
neat nose.

Ned Nott was shot and Sam Shott was not.
So it's better to be Shott than Nott.
Some say Nott was not shot, but Shott swears he
    shot Nott.
Either the shot Shott shot at Nott was not shot or
    Nott was shot.
If the shot Shott shot shot Nott, Nott was shot.
But if the shot Shott shot shot Shott himself,
    then Shott would be shot and Nott would not.
However, the shot Shott shot shot not Shott but
    Nott.
It's not easy to say who was shot and who was not,
    but we know who was Shott and who was Nott.

Needy Noodle nipped his neighbor's nutmegs.
Did Needy Noodle nip his neighbor's nutmegs?
If Needy Noodle nipped his neighbor's nutmegs,
Where are his neighbor's nutmegs that Needy
      Noodle nipped?

Nora's nosy nearsighted niece noisily nibbles
ninety-nine nippy noodles.

There's no need to light a night light
    On a light night like tonight;
For a night light's a slight light
    On a light night like tonight.

O

Oliver Oglethorpe ogled an owl and oyster.
Did Oliver Oglethorpe ogle an owl and oyster?
If Oliver Oglethorpe ogled an owl and oyster,
Where's the owl and oyster Oliver Oglethorpe ogled?

The owner of the Inside Inn
Was outside his Inside Inn,
With his inside outside his Inside Inn.

An oyster met an oyster,
　　And they were oysters two;
Two oysters met two oysters,
　　And they were oysters too;
Four oysters met a pint of milk,
　　And they were oyster stew.

P

The farmer pours pure food for poor mules.

Is there a pleasant peasant's pheasant present?

A pale-pink proud peacock pompously preens
his pleasing, pretty plumage.

Pass the plain pliable painted paper plate, please!

Pat's pa, Pete, poked the pea patch to pick a peck
of peas for the poor pink pig in the pine-pole pen.

Peeved Paul's pop plops a pooped pelican into
the polluted Potomac.

Pearl painfully plays plausible piano.

The pesky pixy picks picnics.

Peter pared the peel from the pile of pears in the pail near the pool, then poked them with a pole.

Peter Piper picked a peck of pickled peppers.
    A peck of pickled peppers Peter Piper picked.
If Peter Piper picked a peck of pickled peppers,
    Where is the peck of pickled peppers
Peter Piper picked?

Pick packed parcel-post packages promptly, please!

A piddling peddler plucked a plump peeled plum from a platter of piled prime purple plums.

Pierre prefers pizza to pretzels.

Plain bun, plum bun, bun without plum.

Please, Paul, pause for proper applause.

Poor peace prospects.

Popular peppy Polly prepares plenty perfectly peppered potatoes.

Pray, place the pleated pressed pants on the plain plank.

Preshrunk shirts.

Priscilla proudly praises poor pure Pierre's plans.

The prize play proves plausible.

A proper pauper pawned a porpoise on purpose.

What prompts pretty prim Patty to primp prettily?

Q

A high I.Q. kid quibbles with quack, quickie quizzes.

One quarter of the quavering quality quail quartet quivers in the quaking quarry.

Quentin quickly quells a quarrel with Quincy.

The quite quiet quaint queen quits quoting questions.

R

A rare rural rodeo really relaxes rustic rustlers.

Red leather, yellow leather.

Remus rammed which real reel wheel?

A right-handed fellow named Wright,
In writing "write" always wrote "rite."
    Where he meant to write right
    If he'd written "write" right,
Wright would not have wrought rot writing "rite."

The rippled rough ruff ruffle ruffles.

Robert Rowley rolled a round roll around.

Robert's robust robot raffles rifles for really
rumpled rubles.

The rough tough bluff ruffian fluffs ruffs.

Rubber baby buggy bumpers.

Rush the washing, Russell.

Randy ransacks a stack of rucksack knapsacks.

See the ragged rugged round robin run round and round the rugged ragged round rabbit.

Who wrongfully rang the wrong ringer recently?

Will real wheels really wheel?

S

A slender cone-shaped spiral-shell sea snail is
called a periwinkle.

Does this shop stock shot silk shorts?

Down the slippery slide they slid
Sitting slightly sideways;
Slipping swiftly, see them skid
On holidays and Fridays.

"Go, my son, and shut the shutter,"
This I heard a mother mutter.
"Shutter's shut," the boy did mutter,
"I can't shut'er any shutter."

I had an old saw,
And I bought a new saw.
I took the handle off the old saw
And put it on the new saw.
And of all the saws
I ever saw,
I never saw a saw saw
Like the new saw sawed.

I saw six small sick slick seals.

I shot three shy thrushes.
You shoot three shy thrushes.

I went into my garden to slay snails.
I saw my little sister slaying snails.
I said, "Hello, my little sister, are
    you slaying snails?
If you slay snails, please slay
    small snails."

If a shipshape ship shop stocks shapely suits,
How many shapely suits would six shipshape ships
    stock,
If each shipshape ship shop stocked
    six shapely suits?

If she stops at the shop where I shop,
And if she shops at the shop where I shop,
Then I surely shan't stop at the shop where she
    shops.

If silly Sally shall shilly-shally, will silly Willy willy-
nilly shilly-shally too?

If the shrimp ship should sink, the shrimp ship
shouldn't sink far from shore.

"Mrs. Smith's Fish Sauce Shop," said the shiny
sign.

Of all the smells I ever smelt, I never smelled a
smelt that smelled as bad as that smelt smelled.

The old school scold
Sold the school coal scuttle:
If the old school scold sold
The school coal scuttle,
The school should scold
And scuttle the old school scold.

Sally Swim saw Sadie Slee
    Slowly, sadly swinging.
"She seems sorrowful," said she.
    So she started singing.
Sadie smiled: soon swiftly swung;
    Sitting straight, steered swiftly.
"Sol," said Sally, "something sung
    scatters sunshine swiftly!"

Sarah saw six slick, slender sycamore saplings.

Sascha slashes sheets slightly.

The sea ceaseth but sufficeth us.

The seething sea ceaseth seething.

A selfish shellfish smelt a stale fish.
If the stale fish was a smelt,
Then the selfish shellfish smelt a smelt.

The shaky shed sheds sheets of sheer shale.

Shall shameless shepherds shampoo shy sheep?

Shall Sherry share such soft shimmering satins?

Shallow sailing ships should surely shun shallow shoals.

She saw thirty-four swift sloops swing shoreward, before she saw forty-three spaceships soar.

She sawed such shoddy seesaws as soon as she saw
Sue saw shoddier seesaws.

She says she shall sew a sheet shut.

She seeks six sick thick thrushes.

She sells seashells by the seashore.
The shells she sells are seashells, I'm sure.
So if she sells seashells by the seashore,
I'm sure she sells seashore shells.

She sits and shells.
She shells and sits.

She slowly sights slight Sam.

She stood by the shimmering, shaking, shoe-shaped
shoe shop sign, warmly welcoming him in.

Sheep shouldn't sleep in a shack;
Sheep should sleep in a shed.

Sheila seldom sells shelled shrimps.

The sheriff should shoot slowly.

Sherry sheds her sheared sheepskin shoulder-shawl.

The shimmering seashore sun shows some sunshine.

The ship's shop ships shiny short shingles.

The shipshape ship shipped slipshod shoes.

A shirt should soon shrink in such suds.

The shivering sheriff shows a shiny, shot shield.

The shoddy shanty shelter shan't shelter Sheila's
short shorn sheep.

The shoe shop shows sharp sharkskin shoes.

Shoppers flocking shopping,
Shocking shoppers shopping.

The short-winded short shortstop shouts shortly.

Should she sell sheer sheets or should she shelve
shaggy shawls?

Should Shirley share her shortcake with sharp
Sherman, or should Shirley share her shaped sherbet
with shy Herman?

Should such a shapeless sash such shabby stitches
show?

Shouldn't sharp soldiers shoot such shells?

Shy Susie Shipton sewed the seams of Sammy's
sharp Sunday shirt.

A sick sparrow sings several showy songs sheltering
under a shaded shrub with shirking sheep.

Silly Sally swiftly shooed seven silly sheep,
The seven silly sheep Silly Sally shoed
Shilly-shallied south.

Sister Susie's sewing shirts for soldiers.

Six short saplings.

Six sick soldiers sighted seven slowly sinking ships.

Six silly sisters selling silk to six sickly seniors.

Six slippery snakes slide slowly south.

Six steaming sheikhs, sitting stitching sheets.

Six thick thistle sticks.

Six sulky sisters shun six suitors.

The sixth sick sheikh's sixth sheep's sick.

Sixty sticky thick things.

Sixty-seven smiling sisters
Sitting in the sunshine singing songs
And chewing cheese.

Sixty-six Swiss ships swiftly shift.

Sixty-six brave maids sat on sixty-six broad beds
and braided sixty-six broad braids.

The sizzling sun shines on several shapely sailing
ships.

A skunk sat on a stump:
The stump thunk the skunk stunk,
The skunk thunk the stump stunk.

The sleepless sleeper seeks sleep.

The slender sleek sloop slopes slowly.

The slight shed slips.

Slim Sam shaved six slippery chins in six seconds.

Slippery seals slipping silently ashore.

Slobs shop in cheap plain slop sop shops.

A sloppy skier slides on slick ski slopes.

A slow sleet slushes streets.

The slowly slit sack sags slightly.

Some say sweet-scented shaving soap should
soothe sore skins.

Some shun sunshine.
Do you shun sunshine?

Some soldiers' shoulders shudder when shrill
shells shriek.

Sometimes she thinks such soft thoughts.

The son ships shipshape sheep soon.

Sooty Sukey
    Shook some soot
From sister Susie's
    Sooty shoes.

A sort of short soldier shoots straight.

A spare spark plug sparks plenty sparks.

Stalk six sick stags silently.

Strict, strong Stephen Stringer
Snared slickly six sickly,
Silky snakes.

Stu chooses stew Tuesday, since Tuesday is Stu's
stew day.

Suddenly swerving, seven small swans
Swam silently southward,
Seeing six swift sailboats
Sailing sedately seaward.

Sue sips subtle super supper soup.

Sugar sacks should be shaken soundly.

The suitor wore shorts and a short shooting suit
    To a short shoot.
But the shorts didn't suit the short shooting suit,
And at the short shoot the short shooting suit
    Didn't suit. Oh, shoot!

The sun shines on the shop signs.

Susan shineth shoes and socks,
Socks and shoes shines Susan;
She ceaseth shining shoes and socks,
For shoes and socks shock Susan.

Susie's shirt shop sells preshrunk shirts.

Swan swam over the sea;
    Swim, swan, swim.
Swan swam back again;
    Well swum, swan.

They sight a sea serpent slay slight seals.

Why should slow sharks shock shipwrecked sailors?

T

Do you think thick thinkers tinker?

Ted threw Fred three free throws.

Ten tidy droll trolls trying to train their troop to
trill two true tunes.

Ten tiny tin tooters tutored ten tiny tin tooters
to toot toots, too.

Ten tongue-tied tailors twisted tinted
    thistles with their teeth.
If ten tongue-tied tailors twisted tinted
    thistles with their teeth,
Who tinted the tinted thistles that the ten
    tongue-tied tailors twisted?

Thalia's sore throat throbs and thumps.

Theodore thought he thrashed the thickest
thickset thug Thursday.

Theophilus Thistle, the successful thistle-sifter,
While sifting a sieve of unsifted thistles,
Thrust three thousand thistles through the thick
    of his thumb.

Thelma sings the same singsong theme song
through.

Theodore's third-thickest thicket thrives.

They threw three thick things.

Thin-skinned Sue threatens to thwack Sam's thigh.

This thistle seems like that thistle.

Those thrushes thrust in thirty thorny thickets thrill throngs.

Three free thugs set three thugs free.

Thriving Theodore Thadwick sells tricky theater trinkets.

Thrust the throbbing thumb in the tubby thimble.

Tie thy thick sock thigh thongs thoroughly.

Tim's ticktock black clock ticks.

Tom threw Tim three thumb tacks.

Tommy Tickle's teacher tickled Tommy.
Where did Tommy Tickle's teacher tickle Tommy?

Try a trio of tough, tricky, truly ticklish tongue twisters tonight.

A tutor who tooted a flute
Tried to tutor two tooters to toot.
    Said the two to the tutor,
    "Is it harder to toot
Or to tutor two tooters to toot?"

A top tough top cop.

Trip a trim twin-track tape recorder.

Truly rural, purely plural, truly rurally, purely
plurally.

Try two twin trains traveling together.

Twenty tinkers took two hundred tin tacks
    to Toy Town.
If twenty tinkers took two hundred tin tacks
    to Toy Town,
How many tin tacks did each of twenty tinkers
    going to Toy Town take?

Twin-screw steel cruisers.

A twister of twists once twisted a twist,
And the twist he was twisting was a three-twisted
twist.
And untwisting this twist one became untwisted,
And untwisted the twist that the twister was
twisting.

'Twixt six thick thumbs stick six thick sticks.

Two tree toads tied together tried to trill as they
trotted to town.

U

An undertaker undertook to undertake an undertaking. The undertaking that the undertaker undertook to undertake was the hardest undertaking the undertaker ever undertook to undertake.

"Under the other udder," uttered the mother otter.

Unique New York.

V

Valiant Vera views very varied vivid volcanoes.

The veteran ventriloquist veterinarian violently vetoes votes.

Vicious, veiled Venetians visit various violent vampires and vultures in vile voodoo vaults.

A vulgar, vague velvet valentine.

W

Billy Wood said he would carry the wood through the wood, and if Wood said he would, Wood would.

I wonder where one wonderful woeful werewolf wanders?

I wish I hadn't washed this wristwatch.
    I've washed all the wheels and works.
This wristwatch which was washed,
    Oh, how it jumps and jerks!

If a warmly warbling warbler warbles to another
warmly warbling warbler, which warmly warbling
warbler warbles warmer?

How much wood would a woodchuck chuck,
    If a woodchuck could chuck wood?
He would chuck, he would, as much as he could,
    If a woodchuck could chuck wood.

If two witches were watching two watches,
which witch would watch which watch?

A waif awakened and weakly wailed wanting water.

Wandering war-weary warriors worry.

Warren's warped wrap wore well.

What whim caused Whitney Whimple to whistle
on the wharf where a floundering whale might
wheel and whirl?

Whether the weather be fine
    Or whether the weather be not;
Whether the weather be cold
    Or whether the weather be hot;
We'll weather the weather
    Whatever the weather,
Whether we like it or not.

Which wishy-washy washerwoman wishes to wash
wash Wednesday?

Which is the witch that wished the wicked wish?

Which rich wretch fetches the catch?

Which wristwatches are Swiss wristwatches?

Who washed Washington's white woolen underwear when Washington's washerwoman went west?

Why does the wristwatch-strap shop shut?

The wily whale wails while well.

Will the wide, wild wig wiggle or wriggle?

Will the wretched wrangler wreck wrench racks?

Will Willis whisper witless words willingly to wary
Willy, or won't he?

Wilson whittles well-whittled wood whittle by whittle.

Wise widowers woo witty widows.

The whitewashed witch watched a walrus winding
white wool.

X

Ex-disk jockey.

X-ray checks clear chests.

Xenia, Xavier, and Xerxes zoom zanily.

Xmas wrecks perplex and vex.

Y

The local yokel's yoked yak yawns.

Yellow leather feather.

Yoga, yeast, and yogurt for Yvonne's youthful yogi.

Yonder Yankee yokel yodels.

Young Yolanda yanks your yo-yo.

Z

This is a zither.

The zany zoo's zesty zebra zigzags with zeal.

Zithers slither slowly.

Zizzi's zippy zipper zips.

7/12/79

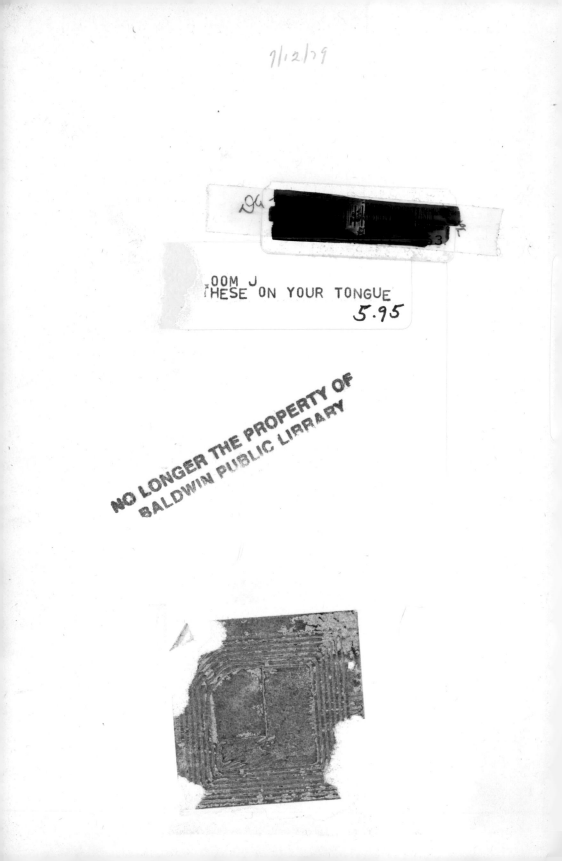